SWAMI
VIVEKANANDA

www.pegasusforkids.com

Published by Kuldeep Jain for B. Jain Publishers (P) Ltd., D-157, Sector 63, Noida - 201307, U.P
Registered office: 1921/10, Chuna Mandi, Paharganj, New Delhi-110055

Printed in India

Contents

4 Who was Swami Vivekananda?

6 Early Years

12 Character of Young Naren

17 Education and Gaining Knowledge

22 Association with Ramakrishna

30 Beginning of Ramakrishna Mission

36 Discovery of Real India

42 The Parliament of Religions

56 Visit to London

58 Sister Nivedita

61 Death of Vivekananda

63 Timeline

65 Activities

68 Glossary

Who was Swami Vivekananda?

Swami Vivekananda, known as Narendranath Datta in his pre-monastic life, was born in an affluent family in Calcutta (now Kolkata) on 12 January 1863. His father was a successful attorney while his mother was endowed with deep devotion, strong character and other remarkable qualities of a fine human being.

As a child, Vivekananda excelled in music, gymnastics and education. By the time he graduated from the University of Kolkata, he had a firm hold on various subjects, especially Western philosophy and history. A man of yogic temperament, he used to practise yoga from his boyhood.

It was at the threshold of youth that Vivekananda passed through a state of spiritual crisis and was assailed by doubts about the existence of God. It was during this phase that he heard about Sri Ramakrishna. In November 1881, Vivekananda went to meet Sri Ramakrishna, who was staying at the Kali Temple in Dakshineshwar.

Sri Ramakrishna not only helped remove doubts from the mind of Vivekananda but also won him over with his unselfish, pure love. This led to a guru-disciple relationship that remains unique in the history of spiritual masters.

Vivekananda was perhaps the first person to introduce the Indian philosophies of Vedanta and Yoga to the Western world. He is also credited with bringing Hinduism to the status of a major world religion during the late 19th century. Vivekananda is considered a major force in the revival of Hinduism in India, and was one who greatly contributed to the concept of nationalism in colonial India. He founded the Ramakrishna Math and the Ramakrishna Mission. He is best known for his speech in Chicago in the Parliament of Religions where he won the hearts of Americans by beginning his speech, "Sisters and brothers of America."

Early Years

Swami Vivekananda, the great soul loved and revered in East and West alike, was born on January 12, 1863. It was the day of the great Hindu festival Makarasamkranti. So, Vivekananda breathed his first amidst the prayers and religious music of thousands of Hindu men and women. He was named Narendranath.

His father, Vishwanath Datta, was an attorney with interests in a wide range of subjects. His mother, Bhuvaneshwari Devi, was a woman of strong character with great spiritual leanings. A boy of great talent, Narendranath was as good in music and gymnastics as he was in studies. Before Narendranath was born, his mother, like many other pious Hindu mothers of that time, had observed religious vows, fasted, and prayed so that she might be blessed with a son, who would bring honour to the family. She requested a relative, who was living in Varanasi, to offer special worship to the Vireswara Shiva of that holy place and seek His blessings. One night she dreamt of Vireswara Shiva arousing Himself from His meditation and agreeing to be born as her son. When she woke up, she was filled with joy.

The Datta family of Calcutta, into which Narendranath had been born, was well known for its affluence, philanthropy, scholarship, and independent spirit. Narendranath grew up to be a sweet, sunny-tempered boy, but very restless. Two governesses were necessary to keep his exuberant energy under control. In order to quieten him, his mother often put his head under the cold-water tap, chanting the name of Lord Shiva; and this miraculously made him peaceful. Narendranath possessed a strong love for birds and animals, and this characteristic reappeared during the last days of his life. Among his boyhood pets were a family cow, a monkey, a goat, a peacock, and several pigeons and guinea-pigs.

He adored the coachman of the family, with his turban, whip, and bright-coloured livery. The coachman was his boyhood ideal of a magnificent person. Narendranath often dreamt to be like him when he grew up! The young boy had developed a special fancy for wandering monks, whose very sight would greatly excite him. One day, when such a monk appeared at his doorstep and asked for alms, Narendranath gave him his only possession, the tiny piece of new cloth that was wrapped round his waist. After this incident, whenever a monk was seen in the neighbourhood, the family would lock up Narendranath in his room. Nevertheless, he would throw out of the window whatever he found near at hand as an offering to the holy man!

During his childhood, Narendranath, like many other Hindu children of his age, developed a love for the Hindu deities, of whom he had learnt from his mother through various stories. He was particularly attracted by the heroic story of Rama and his faithful wife Sita. At this time, he experienced a strange vision daily, when he was about to fall asleep. After he closed his eyes, he would see between his eyebrows a ball of light of changing colours, which would slowly expand and at last burst, bathing his whole body in a white radiance. Watching this light he would gradually fall asleep. Since it was a daily occurrence, he regarded this incident as common to all people, and was surprised when a friend denied ever having seen such a thing!

Years later, however, his spiritual teacher, Sri Ramakrishna, said to him, "Naren, my boy, do you see a light when you go to sleep?"

Ramakrishna was told that such a vision indicated a great spiritual past. The vision of light remained with Narendranath until the end of his life, though later it lost its regularity and intensity.

While still a child, Narendranath practised meditation with a friend before the image of Lord Shiva. Many a time during meditation, he often became unconscious of the world. On one occasion he saw in a vision a luminous person of serene countenance, who was carrying the staff and water-bowl of a monk. The apparition was about to say something when Narendranath became frightened and left the room. He thought later that perhaps this had been a vision of the Buddha.

Character of Young Naren

From an early age this remarkable boy had no fear or superstition. One of his boyish pranks had been to climb a flowering tree belonging to a neighbour, pluck the flowers, and do other mischief. The owner of the tree, finding his pleadings unheard, once told Narendranath's friends that the tree was guarded by a white-robed ghost who would certainly twist their necks if they disturbed his peace. The boys were frightened and kept away. But Narendranath persuaded them to follow him back. He climbed the tree, enjoying his usual measure of fun. Turning to his friends, he said, "What fools you all are! See, my neck is still there. The old man's story is simply not true. Don't believe what others say unless you yourselves know it to be true."

While in school he was the undisputed leader. While playing his favourite game of 'King and the Court,' he would assume the role of the monarch and assign to his friends the roles of the ministers and other state officials. He was destined from birth to lead.

From an early age, Narendranath questioned why one human being should be considered superior to another. In his father's office, separate tobacco pipes were provided for clients belonging to different castes, as orthodox Hindu customs required at that time. Young Narendranath once smoked tobacco from all the pipes, including the one marked for the Muslims. When he was scolded he said, "I wanted to see what happens if I smoke the pipe for Muslims and nothing happened to me!"

During early years, Narendranath's future personality was influenced by his gifted father and his saintly mother, both of whom kept a chastening eye upon him.

On one occasion, he had asked his father, "How shall I conduct myself in the world?"

"Never show surprise at anything," his father had replied.

This priceless advice enabled Narendranath, in his future life, to preserve his peace of mind whether living with princes in their palaces or sharing the straw huts of beggars.

His mother, Bhuvaneswari Devi, played her part in bringing out Narendranath's innate virtues.

"Always follow the truth without caring about the result. Very often you may have to suffer injustice or unpleasant consequences for holding on to the truth; but you must not, under any circumstances, abandon it."

Many years later, Narendranath proudly said to an audience, "I am indebted to my mother for whatever knowledge I have acquired."

Education and Gaining Knowledge

At the age of six, Narendranath was sent to a primary school. One day, however, he repeated at home some of the vulgar words that he had learnt from his classmates. As a result, a private tutor was appointed, who conducted classes for him at home with some other children of the neighbourhood in the worship hall of the house. Narendranath at this point displayed his sharp mind and developed a keen memory.

In 1871, at the age of eight, Narendranath entered high school. His exceptional intelligence was soon recognized by his teachers and classmates. Though at first reluctant to study English because of its foreign origin, he soon took it up. However, the curriculum consumed very little of his time. He used most of his inexhaustible energy in outdoor activities.

In 1879, the family returned to Kolkata from Raipur after a long stay. Narendranath, within a short time, graduated from high school in first division. In the meantime, he had read a great many standard books of English and Bengali literature. History was his favourite subject.

Soon the excitement of his boyhood days was over, and in 1879 Narendranath entered the Presidency College of Kolkata for higher studies. After a year he joined the General Assembly's Institution, founded by the Scottish General Missionary Board, which was later known as the Scottish Church College. It was from Professor Hastie,

Principal of the college and professor of English literature, that Naren first heard the name Sri Ramakrishna.

In college, Narendranath enjoyed serious studies. During the first two years he studied Western logic. Thereafter, he specialized in Western philosophy and the Ancient and Modern History of the different European nations. His memory was prodigious. It took him only three days to assimilate *Green's History of the English People*. Often, on the eve of an examination, he would read the whole night, keeping awake by drinking strong tea or coffee.

Narendranath was a multifaceted genius. He studied both instrumental and vocal music under expert teachers. He could play many instruments with ease, but excelled in singing. From a Muslim teacher he learnt Hindi, Urdu, and Persian songs, most of them of devotional nature.

He also became associated with the Brahmo Samaj, an important religious movement of the time, which influenced him during this formative period of his life.

The Brahmo Samaj, especially captured the imagination of the educated youth of Bengal. Raja Ram Mohan Roy, the founder of this religious organization, broke away from the rituals, image worship, and priestcraft of orthodox Hinduism and exhorted his followers to dedicate themselves to the 'worship and adoration of the Eternal, the Unsearchable, who is the Author and the Preserver of the universe.'

Raja Ram Mohan Roy, endowed with a rich intellect, was the first Indian to realize the importance of Western education. Hence, he took active part in the introduction of English education in India.

Association with Ramakrishna

About this time, Narendranath came in contact with Sri Ramakrishna, the apparently illiterate but learned saint. This event was to become the major turning point of his life. As a result of his association with Sri Ramakrishna, Naren's innate spiritual yearning stirred up, and he began to feel the transitoriness of the world and the futility of academic education. The day before his B.A. examination, he suddenly felt a strong love for God and, standing before the room of a college-mate, sang many devotional songs. His surprised friends, reminded him of the next day's examination, but Narendranath was unconcerned. It was as if the shadow of the approaching monastic life was fast falling on him. He appeared for the examination, however, and easily got through.

Narendranath met Ramakrishna Paramahamsa for the first time in November 1881, at the house of the Master's devotee Surendranath Mitra. Ramakrishna was much impressed by his sincerity and devotion, and after a few inquiries asked him to visit him at Dakshineswar. Narendranath accepted the invitation as he wished to see if Ramakrishna was the one who could help him in his spiritual quest.

On one occasion, Narendranath asked the Master, "Sir, have you seen God?"

Without a moment's hesitation the reply was given.

"Yes, I have seen God. I see Him as I see you here, only more clearly. God can be seen. One can talk to him. But who cares for God? People shed torrents of tears for their wives, children, wealth, and property, but who weeps for the vision of God? If one cries sincerely for God, one can surely see Him."

Narendranath was astounded. For the first time, he was face to face with a man who asserted that he had seen God! For the first time, in fact, he was hearing that

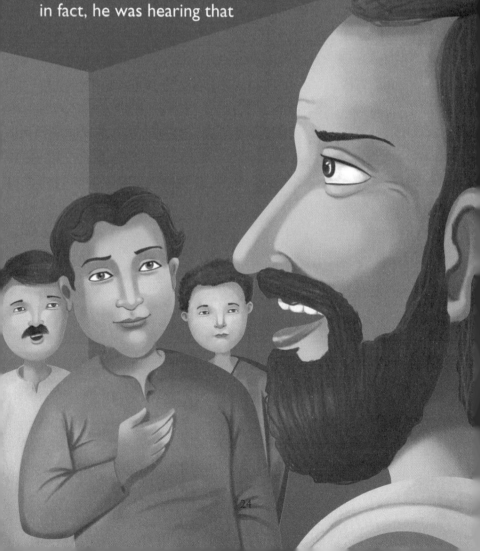

God could be seen. He could feel that Ramakrishna's words were uttered from the depths of an inner experience. They could not be doubted. Still he could not reconcile these words with Ramakrishna's strange conduct, which he had witnessed only a few minutes before. What puzzled Narendranath further was Ramakrishna's normal behaviour in the presence of others. The young man returned to Kolkata bewildered, but with a feeling of inner peace.

During his second visit to the Master, Narendranath had an even stranger experience. After a minute or two, Ramakrishna drew near him in an ecstatic mood, muttered a few words, fixed his eyes on him, and placed his right foot on Narendranath's chest. At this touch Narendranath saw, with eyes open, the walls, the room, the temple garden, in fact the whole world, vanishing, and even himself disappearing into a void. He felt sure that he was facing death.

He cried, "What are you doing to me? I have my parents, brothers, and sisters at home."

The Master laughed and stroked Narendranath's chest, restoring him to his normal mood. He said, "All right, everything will happen in due time."

Narendranath was bewildered. He felt that Ramakrishna had cast a hypnotic spell upon him. But how could that have been? He felt disgusted that he was unable to resist the influence of a madman. Nevertheless, he felt a great inner attraction for Ramakrishna.

On his third visit, Narendranath fared no better, though he tried his utmost to be on guard. Ramakrishna took him to a neighbouring garden and, in a state of trance, touched him. Completely overwhelmed, Narendranath lost consciousness.

Ramakrishna, referring later to this incident, said that after putting Narendranath into a state of unconsciousness, he had asked him many questions about his past, his mission in the world, and the duration of his present life. The answers had only confirmed what he himself had thought about these matters. Ramakrishna told his other disciples that Narendranath had attained perfection even before this birth; that he was an adept in meditation; and that the day Narendranath recognized his true self, he would give up the body by an act of will, through yoga. Often he was heard saying that Narendranath was one of the 'Saptarshis', or Seven Sages, who live in the realm of the Absolute. He often narrated to others about a vision he had had regarding the disciple's spiritual heritage.

The meeting of Narendranath and Ramakrishna was an important event in the lives of both the great men. A storm had been raging in Narendranath's soul when he came to Ramakrishna, who himself had passed through a similar struggle but was then firmly anchored in peace as a result of his realization of Brahman as the immutable essence of all things.

For five years Narendranath closely watched the Master, never allowing himself to be influenced by blind faith.

He always tested the words and actions of Ramakrishna with reason. It cost him many sorrows and much anguish before he accepted Ramakrishna as his guru and the ideal of the spiritual life. Nevertheless, when the acceptance came, it was wholehearted and final. The Master, too, was overjoyed to find a disciple who reasoned every belief, and he knew that Narendranath was the one who would carry his message to the world.

Ramakrishna never once asked Narendranath to abandon reason. He met the challenge of Narendranath's intellect

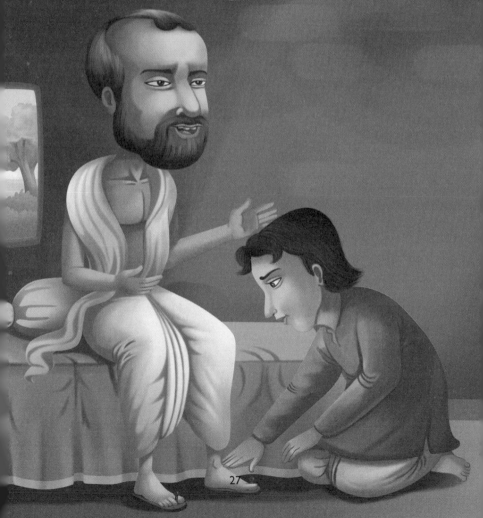

with his superior understanding. When Narendranath's reasoning failed to solve the ultimate mystery, the Master gave him the necessary insight. Thus, with infinite patience, love and vigilance, he tamed the rebellious spirit, demanding complete obedience to moral and spiritual disciplines, without which no religious life can be built on a firm foundation.

Ramakrishna was a perfect teacher. He never laid down identical disciplines for disciples of diverse temperaments. He did not insist that Narendranath should follow strict rules about food, nor did he ask him to believe in the reality of gods and goddesses of Hindu mythology.

However, he would often test Narendranath. One day, when Narendranath entered the Master's room, he was completely ignored. Not a word of greeting was uttered. A week later he came back and met with the same indifference, and during the third and fourth visits saw no evidence of any thawing of the Master's frigid attitude.

At the end of a month, Ramakrishna said to Narendranath, "I have not exchanged a single word with you all this time, and still you come."

The disciple replied, "I come to Dakshineswar because I love you and want to see you. I do not come here to hear your words."

The Master was overjoyed to hear this. Embracing the disciple, he said, "I was only testing you. I wanted to see if you would stay away on account of my outward indifference. Only a man of your inner strength could put up with such indifference on my part. Anyone else would have left me long ago."

During the course of five years of his training under Ramakrishna, Narendranath was transformed from a restless, puzzled, impatient youth to a mature man who was ready to renounce everything for the sake of God realization.

Beginning of Ramakrishna Mission

Ramakrishna left his mortal body on August 16, 1886. Before his death, he had given specific instructions to Narendranath for leading a monastic life.

After the death of Ramakrishna, Narendra and eight other disciples took formal monastic vows. They decided to live their lives as their master did. It was then that Narendranath took the name 'Swami Vivekananda'.

Vivekananda's disciples, under his leadership, formed a fellowship at a half-ruined house at Baranagar, near Kolkata. This became the first building of the Ramakrishna Math. Dreary and dilapidated, it was a building that had the reputation of being haunted by evil spirits. The young disciples were happy to take refuge in it from the turmoil of Kolkata. This 'Baranagore Math', as the new monastery was called, became the first headquarters of the monks of the Ramakrishna Order. Its centre was the shrine room, where the copper vessel containing the sacred ashes of the Master was daily worshipped as his visible presence.

Among the Master's disciples, Tarak, Latu, and Gopal had already cut off their relationship with their families. The young disciples whom Ramakrishna had destined for the monastic life were in need of shelter. The Master had asked Narendranath to see to it that they should not become householders. Narendranath vividly remembered

the Master's dying words, "Narendranath, take care of the boys."

Vivekanada and other members of the 'Math' often spent their time in meditation and discussing different philosophies and teachings of spiritual teachers including

32

Ramakrishna, Adi Shankara, Ramanuja, and Jesus Christ. In January 1899, the Baranagar Math was shifted to a newly acquired plot of land at Belur in the district of Howrah, now famous as the 'Belur Math'. But the problem of bearing expenses of these young disciples still remained. How would they be provided with food and the basic necessities of life?

All these problems were solved by the generosity of Surendranath Mitra, another disciple of Ramakrishna. He came forward to pay the expenses of new quarters for the Master's homeless disciples.

Narendranath devoted himself whole-heartedly to the training of the young brother disciples. He spent the day-time at home, supervising a lawsuit that was pending in the court and looking after certain other family affairs; but during the evenings and nights he was always with his

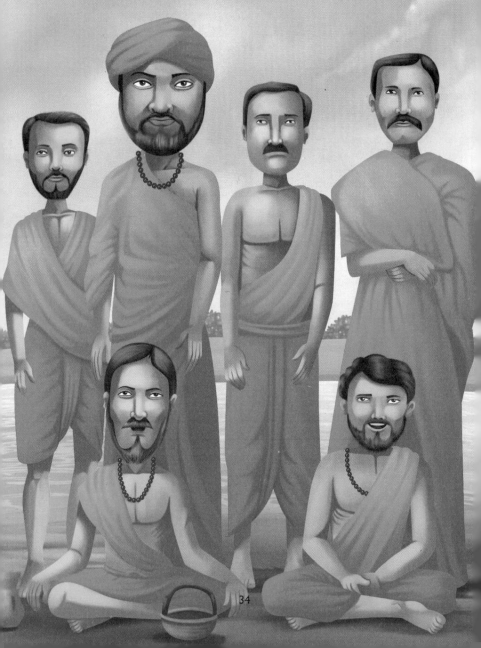

brothers at the monastery, exhorting them to practice spiritual disciplines. His presence was a source of unfailing delight and inspiration to all.

Ramakrishna instilled in these young men the spirit of renunciation and brotherly love for one another.

One day, he distributed ochre robes among them and sent them out to beg food. In this way he himself laid the foundation for a new monastic order.

After establishing the new monastic order, Vivekananda heard the inner call for a greater mission in his life. While most of the followers of Sri Ramakrishna thought of him in relation to their own personal lives, Vivekananda thought of the Master in relation to India and the rest of the world. As the prophet of the present age, what was Ramakrishna's message to the modern world and to India in particular? This question and the awareness of his own inherent powers urged Vivekananda to go out alone into the wide world. In the middle of 1890, after receiving the blessings of Sri Sarada Devi, the divine consort of Sri Ramakrishna and known to the world as Holy Mother, Vivekananda left Baranagar Math and began a long journey of exploration and discovery of India.

Discovery of Real India

In the year 1888, Vivekananda left the 'math' as a 'Parivrâjaka'—the Hindu religious life of a wandering monk. His sole possessions were a 'kamandalu' (water pot), staff, and his two favourite books—'Bhagavad Gita' and 'The Imitation of Christ'. Vivekananda travelled the length and breadth of India for five years, visiting important centres of learning, acquainting himself with the diverse religious traditions and different patterns of social life. He developed sympathy for the suffering and poverty of the masses, and resolved to uplift the nation. Living mainly on 'bhiksha' or alms, Vivekananda travelled mostly on foot and railway tickets

bought by his admirers whom he met during the travels.

During these travels, he gained acquaintance and stayed with scholars, Dewans, Rajas and people from all walks of life—Hindus, Muslims, Christians, Pariahs (low caste workers) and Government officials. In Madurai, he met the Raja of Ramnad, Bhaskara Setupati. The Raja became Vivekananda's disciple and urged him to go to the Parliament of Religions at Chicago. With the aid of funds collected by his Madras disciples and Rajas of Mysore, Ramnad, Khetri, Dewans and other followers, Vivekananda could go to Chicago on May 31, 1893.

During his travels all over India, Vivekananda was deeply moved to see the extreme poverty and backwardness of the masses. He was the first religious leader in India to understand and openly declare that the real cause of India's downfall was the neglect of the masses. The immediate need was to provide food and other bare necessities of life

to the hungry millions. For this, they needed to be taught improved methods of agriculture, village industries, etc.

It was in this context that he grasped the root cause of the problem of poverty in India. It was centuries of oppression. Due to this, the downtrodden masses had lost faith in their own capacity to improve their own lives. He saw that, in spite of poverty, the masses clung to religion, but they had never been taught the life-giving principles of Vedanta and how to apply them in practical life.

Thus, the masses needed two kinds of knowledge— secular knowledge to improve their economic condition and spiritual knowledge to infuse in them faith in themselves and strengthen their moral sense. The next question was how to spread these two kinds of knowledge among the masses? Vivekananda understood that this could only be done through education.

Vivekananda was certain that to carry out his plans for the spread of education and for the upliftment of the poor masses, and also of women, an efficient organization of dedicated people was needed. As he said later on, he wanted "to set in motion machinery which will bring

noblest ideas to the doorstep of even the poorest and the meanest". To serve as this 'machinery', Vivekananda founded the Ramakrishna Mission a few years later.

The Parliament of Religions

It was when these ideas were taking shape in his mind in the course of his wanderings that Vivekananda heard about the World's Parliament of Religions to be held in Chicago in 1893. The Raja of Ramnad, Bhaskara Setupati, who had become his disciple along with a few others, convinced him to attend the Parliament. Vivekananda too felt that the Parliament would provide the right forum to present his views on religion.

Soon after his arrival in Chicago, Vivekananda went to the information bureau of the exposition to ask about the forthcoming Parliament of Religions. He was told that it had been put off until the first week of September. Also, Vivekanada did not have any credentials from a bona fide organization that would enable him to be accepted as a delegate. He was also told that it was anyway too late for him to be registered as a delegate. Vivekananda had expected this for not one of his friends in India—the enthusiastic devotees of Madras, the Raja of Khetri, the Raja of Ramnad, the Maharaja of Mysore, the ministers of the native states, and the disciples who had

arranged his trip to America—had taken the trouble to make any inquiries concerning the details of the Parliament. No one knew the dates of the meetings or the conditions of admission. Nor had Vivekananda brought with him any letter of authority from a religious organization.

In the meantime, the money that Vivekananda had carried from India was dwindling. He did not have enough to sustain him in Chicago until September. In a frantic mood he asked help from the Theosophical Society, which professed warm friendship for India. He was told that he would have to subscribe to the creed of the Society; but this he refused to do because he did not believe in most of the Theosophical doctrines. Hearing this, the leader declined to give him any help. Vivekananda now became desperate and cabled to his friends in Madras for money.

Finally, someone advised him to go to Boston, where the cost of living was cheaper. While he was on his way, he attracted the attention of a wealthy lady who resided in the suburbs of the city. She cordially invited him to be her guest. He accepted the offer to save his dwindling purse. He was lodged at 'Breezy Meadows,' in Metcalf, Massachusetts, and his hostess, Miss Kate Sanborn, was delighted to display to her inquisitive friends this strange man from the Far East. Vivekananda met a number of people, most of whom annoyed him by asking queer questions regarding Hinduism and the social customs of India.

Vivekananda had no friends in the foreign land; yet he did not lose faith. The train bearing Vivekananda to Chicago arrived late in the evening, and he had mislaid, unfortunately, the address of the committee in charge of the delegates. He did not know where to turn for help, and no one bothered to give information to this foreigner of strange appearance. How he finally managed to attend the Parliament is a long tale.

The Parliament of Religions

On Monday, September 11, 1893, the Parliament of Religions opened. This great meeting was an adjunct to the World's Columbian Exposition, which had been organized to celebrate the 400th anniversary of the discovery of America by Christopher Columbus. One of the main goals of the exposition was to disseminate knowledge of the progress and enlightenment brought about in the world by Western savants and especially

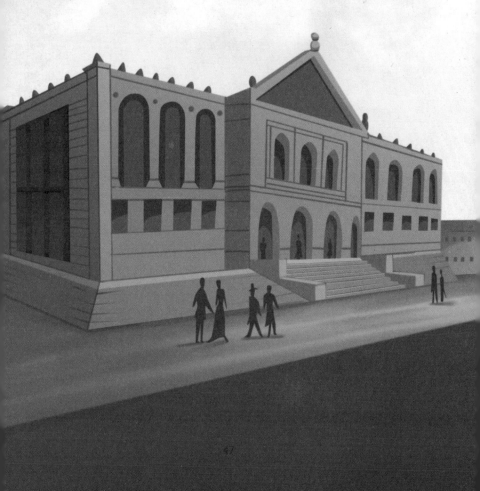

through physical science and technology. But as religion forms a vital factor in human culture, it had been decided to organize a Parliament of Religions in combination with the exposition.

At 10 a.m., the Parliament opened. In it every form of organized religious belief, as professed among twelve hundred million people, was represented. Among the non-Christian groups could be counted Hinduism, Jainism, Buddhism, Confucianism, Shintoism, Mohammedanism, and Mazdaism.

The spacious hall and the huge gallery of the art palace were packed with 7,000 people—men and women representing the culture of the United States.

Vivekananda occupied a chair where on his left and right were grouped the Oriental delegates like Pratap Chandra Mazoomdar of the Calcutta Brahmo Samaj, and Nagarkar of Bombay; Dharmapala, representing the Ceylon Buddhists; Gandhi, representing the Jains; and Chakravarti and Annie Besant from the Theosophical Society. With them sat Swami Vivekananda, who represented no particular sect, but the Universal Religion of the Vedas.

His gorgeous robe, large yellow turban, bronze complexion, and fine features stood out prominently on the platform and drew everyone's notice. In numerical order, Vivekananda's position was number thirty-one. The delegates arose, one by one, and read prepared speeches, but Vivekananda was completely unprepared.

Several times he postponed the summons. At last, he came to the rostrum and Dr. Barrows introduced him. Bowing to Sarasvati, the Indian Goddess of Wisdom, in his mind, Vivekananda addressed the audience as "Sisters and Brothers of America." Instantly, thousands arose in their seats and gave him a loud applause. They were deeply moved to see, at last, a man who discarded formal words and spoke to them with the natural warmth of a brother.

It took full two minutes before the thunderous applause subsided, and Vivekananda began his speech by thanking the youngest of the nations in the name of the most ancient monastic order in the world—the Vedic order of sannyasins. The keynote of his address was universal toleration and acceptance. He told the audience how India, even in olden times, had given shelter to the religious refugees of other lands—for instance, the Israelites and the Zoroastrians. He quoted from the scriptures two passages revealing the Hindu spirit of toleration. The response was deafening applause. It appeared that the whole audience had been patiently awaiting this message of religious harmony.

There was not a word of condemnation for any faith uttered by Vivekananda. He did not believe that this religion or that religion was true in this or that respect. To him, all religions were equally effective paths to lead their respective devotees, with diverse tastes and temperaments, to the same goal of perfection.

Vivekananda addressed the Parliament about a dozen times. His outstanding address was on Hinduism in which he discussed Hindu metaphysics, psychology, theology; the divinity of the soul, the oneness of existence, and the harmony of religions. He taught that the final goal of man is to become divine by realizing the Divine and that human beings are the children of 'Immortal Bliss'.

Newspapers published his speeches and they were read with warm interest all over the country. The New York

Herald said: 'He is undoubtedly the greatest figure in the Parliament of Religions. After hearing him we feel how foolish it is to send missionaries to this learned nation.' The Boston Evening Post said:

'He is a great favourite at the Parliament from the grandeur of his sentiments and his appearance as well. He merely crosses the platform he is applauded; and this marked

approval of thousands he accepts in a childlike spirit of gratification without a trace of conceit....At the Parliament of Religions they used to keep Vivekananda until the end of the programme to make people stay till the end of the session....' The four thousand fanning people in the Hall of Columbus would sit smiling and expectant, waiting for an hour or two to listen to Vivekananda for fifteen minutes. The chairman knew the old rule of keeping the best until the last.

The reports of the Parliament of Religions were published in Indian magazines and newspapers as well. Vivekananda's justifications of the Hindu faith filled with pride the hearts of his countrymen from Colombo to Almora, from Calcutta (Kolkata) to Bombay (Mumbai). The brother monks at the Baranagore monastery were initially not clear about the identity of Vivekananda. A letter from him, six months after the Parliament, removed all doubts, however, and they were proud of Vivekananda's achievement!

After he had delivered his message in the Parliament, Vivekananda suffered no longer from material wants. The doors of the wealthy were thrown open. Vivekananda

had sincere admirers and devotees among the Americans, who looked after his comforts, gave him money when he sensed lack of it, and followed his instructions. Their lavish hospitality made him sick at heart when he remembered the crushing poverty of his own people in India. He was particularly grateful to American women, and wrote many letters to his friends in India paying high praise to their virtues.

He accepted invitation from churches, clubs, and private gatherings, and travelled extensively through the Eastern and Midwestern states of America, delivering twelve to fourteen or more lectures a week.

Visit to London

For some time Vivekananda had been planning a visit to London. He wished to sow the seed of Vedanta in the capital of the mighty British Empire.

Henrietta Müller, a Chilean-British women's rights activist and theosophist, had extended to him a cordial invitation to come to London, while E.T. Sturdy, member of the Theosophical Society, had requested him to stay at his home there. Leggett, too, had invited the Swami to come to Paris as his guest.

After sweeping London with his remarkable speeches, Vivekananda prepared to return. He was given a magnificent farewell by his English friends, devotees and admirers on December 13 at the Royal Society of Painters in Water-Colours, in Piccadilly. Around 500 people gathered at the farewell. While some were silent, tongue-tied and sad at heart, others were teary eyed.

Sister Nivedita

It was in the month of November 1895 that Vivekananda met Margaret Noble for the first time. She was later to become his most devoted disciple by the name of Sister Nivedita. During his second visit, in 1896, the bond between the two became irrevocable.

Margaret Noble was a versatile genius. She was the most respected disciple of Swami Vivekananda. She was a revolutionary, a lover of modern science, arts, and philosophy, and stood for the emancipation of Indian women.

Margaret was Irish by birth but became a true Indian; her love for India was incomparable. She was a social worker, author and a teacher.

She spent her childhood and early days of her youth in Ireland. From her father and from her college professor, she imbibed many valuable lessons, the most important being service to mankind is the true service to God.

Renamed fondly by Vivekananda, Sister Nivedita (meaning one who is dedicated to God) came to Kolkata in the year 1898. Vivekananda initiated her into the vow of 'brahmacharya' on March 25, 1898. In November 1898, she opened a girls' school in Bagbazar area of Kolkata. She wanted to educate girls who were deprived of even basic education. During the plague epidemic in Kolkata in 1899, Sister Nivedita nursed and took care of the poor patients.

Sister Nivedita had close associations with the newly established Ramakrishna Mission. She had actively contributed to Indian nationalism as well. She was very intimate with Sarada Devi, the spiritual consort of Ramakrishna and one of the major influences behind

Ramakrishna Mission, and also with all brother disciples of Swami Vivekananda. She died on October 13, 1911, in Darjeeling. Her epitaph reads: 'Here reposes Sister Nivedita who gave her all to India.'

Death of Vivekananda

Vivekananda was often heard saying that he would not live to be 40. He left his mortal body on July 4, 1902.

On his last day, he performed all his duties like every day and ate with his fellow sanyasis with great relish. At 7 o'clock in the evening, the bell rang for worship in the temple. Vivekananda went to his room and told the disciple who attended him that none was to come to him until called for. He spent an hour in meditation and then called the disciple and asked him to open all the windows and fan his head. He lay down quietly on his bed and the attendant thought that he was either sleeping or meditating.

At the end of an hour, his hands began to tremble and he breathed once very deeply. There was silence for a minute

or two, and again he breathed in the same manner. His eyes became fixed in the centre of his eyebrows, his face assumed a divine expression, and eternal silence fell.

Swami Vivekananda passed away at the age of 39, thus fulfilling his own prophecy, "I shall not live to be 40 years old."

- 1863 Swami Vivekananda is born on January 12, in Calcutta

- 1869 He starts education in a 'pathshala'

- 1871 Vivekananda joins Pandit Vidyasagar's school

- 1877 He goes to Raipur to study

- 1879 Vivekananda goes back to Calcutta and joins the same school, where he passes entrance examination (matriculation)

- 1880 He joins the Arts section of Presidency College

- 1881 He passes FA examination (Higher Secondary, Class XII) from Scottish Church College; he continues his BA studies in the same institution

- 1881 Vivekananda meets Ramakrishna for the first time in November in Calcutta; they meet at the house of Surendranath Mitra

  Ramkrishna tells Vivekananda that he has seen God

- 1884 Vivekananda passes Bachelor of Arts examination from Scottish Church College

- 1886 Ramakrishna passes away on August 15

  The monks take up a new residence at a small monastery they establish in Baranagore

  At Baranagore, 12 monks take oath of allegiance and form a new order, their motto being working for the emancipation of the world

- 1893 Vivekananda begins his journey to America from Bombay on May 31, after bidding goodbye to his fellow monks

Class Discussion

Initiate a class discussion on a few religious leaders of the world. They may belong to any country or any religion. Discuss and highlight how they have been a source of inspiration to us.

Research Work

Find out about Ramakrishna Mission—how it came into being, who began it, what is the nature of its work, etc. Collect pictures and information from the internet and make a project in a scrap file.

Group Activity

Form groups of five or six and discuss what service means to each of you. Talk about how you can deliver service to your society and country at large as a student. Make a list of small acts of kindness that can help people around you and help to spread a good feeling of co-operation.

Activities

Activities

1. Who was Swami Vivekananda?

2. When was he born?

3. What was his name given by his family?

4. Name his parents.

5. Describe the character of Vivekananda.

6. How do you know that Vivekananda was highly impressed with monks?

7. Whom did Vivekananda accept as his guru? Why?

8. What was Vivekananda's favourite subject in school?

9. How do you know that Vivekananda was a multifaceted genius?

10. Where did Vivekananda meet Ramakrishna Paramahamsa?

11. Why was Vivekananda astounded when they met?

12. Describe how the organization of Ramakrishna Mission began?

13. When Vivekananda travelled throughout India, what did he observe?

14. When and where was the Parliament of Religions held?

15. Who funded Vivekananda to attend it?

16. Describe the hardships he faced there.

17. How did Vivekananda win the hearts of the thousands of Americans through his speech?

18. What was the result of his speech at the Parliament of Religions?

19. Who was Margaret Noble?

20. How does Vivekananda inspire us?

Glossary

admirer: someone who has high regard for someone or something

affluence: wealthy

apparition: a ghost-like image of a person

astounded: to be shocked greatly

bewildered: greatly confused

brahmacharya: a virtuous lifestyle that also includes simple living, meditation and other behaviors

chastening: to correct by punishment

condemnation: to express strong disapproval

conjunction: two or more events or things occurring at the same point in time

curriculum: the subjects comprising a course of study

dedicated: devoted to a task

delegate: a person sent to a conference as an authorized representative

deprived: one who lacks basic material benefits

devotee: a strong believer in a particular religion or god

devotional: used in religious worship

dilapidated: an old building or object in a state of ruin

disciple: a follower or pupil of a teacher or a leader

disseminate: to scatter or spread widely

divine: godly

duration: the time taken for something

dwindling: gradually decreasing in size, amount, or strength

emancipation: the process of setting free from legal, social, or political compulsions

epitaph: a phrase or form of words written in memory of a person who has died

expectant: a feeling of excitement that something is about to happen

expenses: the cost incurred for something

exposition: a comprehensive explanation of an idea

exuberant: full of energy and excitement

frigid: icy, cold

gorgeous: very attractive; praise expressed by clapping

grandeur: majestic and impressive

hospitality: friendly and generous reception given to guests or visitors

hypnotic: something related to hypnosis

ignore: to refuse to take notice of someone or something

indifference: lack of interest or concern

injustice: lack of fairness

instilled: to gradually but firmly establish something in someone's mind

irrevocable: not able to be changed or reversed

justifications: to show that something is right or reasonable

magnificent: extremely beautiful

Makarasamkranti: a Hindu harvest festival celebrated in various parts of India and Nepal

meditation: the action of meditating or reflecting

metaphysics: a branch of philosophy

miraculously: an unusual event that cannot be explained by scientific laws

mischief: a playful misbehaviour

monarch: a head of state like a king, queen, or emperor

mortal: one who is subject to death

mystery: something that is difficult to understand or explain

oppression: cruel or unjust treatment for a long time

overwhelmed: having a strong emotional effect

pious: holy, religious

possessions: the state of owning something

poverty: lack of money or wealth

priestcraft: the knowledge and work of a priest

prophecy: a prediction of future

prophet: a person regarded as an inspired teacher of the will of God

psychology: the scientific study of the human mind and its functions

puzzled: unable to understand

rebellious: one who resists authority

relish: pleasurable anticipation of something

renunciation: to formally reject something

sanyasin: a Hindu religious mendicant

scold: to rebuke someone angrily

stirred: arouse strong feeling in someone

superior: higher in rank or status

superstition: an irrational belief

theology: the study of the nature of God and religious beliefs

Theosophical Society: an organization formed in 1875 for the advancement of theosophy

Glossary

thunderous: very loud

transform: to make a marked change

transitoriness: not permanent

unconscious: not awake and aware of

unpleasant: something that causes discomfort or unhappiness

unsearchable: something that cannot be searched or understood

vigilance: the action or state of keeping careful watch over something

vulgar: lacking good taste

wrapped: to arrange or fold something as cover or protection